Unique Journey with Autism:

A Guide to Understanding, Empowering, and Embracing Autism

By

Leila J. Pittman

Table of Contents

Introduction

There is a wonderful spectrum of diversity that refuses to conform despite the fact that we live in a culture that frequently tries to force individuals to fit into predetermined moulds. One of these facets of this colourful tapestry of human existence is autism, a condition that affects the brain in a complex way. Nevertheless, it is a tapestry that many of us have not yet reached a point where we can fully comprehend, value, and accept.

Through reading this book, "Unique Journey with Autism," you will be taken on a trip that is both educational and eye-opening. It is a voyage that goes beyond generalizations and busts myths, providing a deeper and more empathetic knowledge of autism and the wonderful people who live in this one-of-a-kind world.

In the following paragraphs, we will delve into the intricacies of autism and investigate its many characteristics, as well as the difficulties and advantages associated with them. We will listen to the experiences of autistic people, as well as parents, carers, and advocates who have devoted their lives to understanding the complexities of autism and working towards a society in which acceptance and inclusion are prioritized. These individuals have worked tirelessly to promote a world in which autistic people are treated with dignity and respect.

The book "Unique Journey with Autism" is more than just a book; it is a bridge. It is a bridge connecting hearts and minds, cultivating empathy, and encouraging a brighter future in which everyone, regardless of their neurodiversity, can grow and contribute to the rich tapestry of mankind.

As we go out on this adventure together, let us cast aside any preconceived beliefs and instead welcome the diversity that contributes to the wondrous and singular character of our world. We have the ability to create a world in which every individual, regardless of where they lie on the spectrum of ability, is honoured and respected for the extraordinary gift that they are if we have the understanding, acceptance, and empowerment necessary

Chapter 1: Understanding Autism

In a world that values variety, it is essential to lift the veil of misunderstanding that has so frequently clouded our perception of autism. This is especially true in the medical community. In this chapter, we will begin on a journey to expose the essence of autism. We will explore past the preconceptions and myths that have obscured our image of autism, and we will discover the colourful, complicated reality that lies beneath the surface.

Definition of Autism: Beyond the Common Misconceptions

Autism is not a single condition that can be defined in a way that is applicable to all cases. It can be seen as a spectrum, a large and complex mosaic of features that varies from person to person. It is a condition that changes the way people see the world around them and how they interact with it. As a result, it has an effect on people's ideas, feelings, and behaviours.

When attempting to characterize autism, it is necessary to first recognize its diversity and the fact that no two autistic people are identical to one another. It is important to recognize that autism involves a diverse set of skills and difficulties, as well as strengths and shortcomings. To embrace this is to acknowledge that autism is a normal component of the human experience and an essential component of the social fabric of our modern world.

Autism's Spectrum: A Complex Reality

The term "spectrum" was coined to describe the diverse range of experiences and characteristics that are included in the diagnostic category of autism. On one end of this spectrum, we find people who may need significant assistance in their day-to-day lives. On the other end, we have people who thrive in particular areas and frequently demonstrate amazing gifts or abilities.

The spectrum, on the other hand, is not a linear scale; rather, it is more analogous to a kaleidoscope, in which each individual possesses a distinctive arrangement of colours and shapes. Some people may have difficulty communicating and interacting with others, while others may have remarkable aptitude in areas such as mathematics, music, or the arts. Some people may have sensitivities that make some situations overwhelming for them, whilst other people may take pleasure in the world's varied and abundant sensory experiences.

The Neurodiversity Framework
In order to make progress in our understanding of autism, it is imperative that we acknowledge the existence of neurodiversity. This paradigm acknowledges that neurological variances, such as autism, are inherent variations of the human brain. Specifically, it focuses on autism. Neurodiversity contributes to the enrichment of our society by providing a wide range of viewpoints, abilities, and gifts, much as biodiversity is essential to the well-being of our ecosystems.

Instead of viewing autism as a "disorder" that needs to be treated or cured, the neurodiversity paradigm encourages us to appreciate and accommodate these distinctions rather than portraying autism as a problem that has to be solved. It motivates us to cultivate circumstances that enable autistic individuals to flourish, to give their one-of-a-kind gifts to our communities, and to live fulfilling lives on their own terms, as well as to establish spaces where they can do so independently.

In the next chapters, we will continue to unveil the layers of autism, revealing its many characteristics and exploring the ways in which we may assist autistic individuals and give them the empowerment they need to lead meaningful lives. But first, let us get rid of whatever preconceived views we may have about autism and approach it with an open heart and a readiness to learn since it is only when we understand the truth that we will be able to genuinely appreciate the wonderful qualities of autism.

Chapter 2: Early Symptoms and Diagnosis

The journey towards understanding and accepting autism frequently starts with the identification of early indicators and the process of getting a diagnosis. In this chapter, we discuss how to recognize the subtle signs and features that may suggest autism in young children. These cues and qualities might be difficult to spot in young children. In addition to this, we are going to look into the emotional journey that many parents and other carers go through while they are trying to get a diagnosis for their child.

Identifying Early Signs

Autism is a syndrome that frequently manifests itself in early life, typically before the age of three. However, the signals may appear in a variety of ways depending on the child. It is essential to keep in mind that not all developmental differences are indicative of autism; however, there are a few frequent early warning indicators that parents and other carers should be on the lookout for:

Problems in Social Relationships: Autism is known to cause difficulties in social relationships for many young children. It's possible that they won't make eye contact with you, won't reply when you call their name, or won't be able to hold a normal conversation.

Communication Difficulties: A prominent early sign of communication difficulties is a delay in the development of speech or language. Some autistic children do not talk at all, while others may have limited language skills or use language in unusual ways. However, all autistic children have difficulties communicating in some way.

Repetitive behaviours: Children with autism frequently engage in repetitive behaviours or routines. These behaviours can be either verbal or nonverbal. These behaviours can include rocking back and forth, flapping one's hands, or getting concentrated on a particular object or area of interest.

Sensitivity to Sensory Input: Autistic children may have heightened sensitivity to many types of sensory input. They may have an extreme sensitivity to particular sensory stimuli, such as loud noises or particular textures, or they may actively seek out sensory input, such as spinning or swinging.

Difficulty with routines: Changes in routines or transitions from one activity to another can be problematic for autistic children. This can also apply to transitions between different types of activities. When confronted with unanticipated shifts, they could become agitated or even have a meltdown.

The Methods Used in the Diagnosis

If a parent or other carer notices any of these early warning indicators, it is imperative that they seek help from a professional. A thorough assessment by medical professionals, who may typically include developmental paediatricians, child psychologists, or neurologists, is required for the process of making a diagnosis.

This assessment might include the following:

Medical History: An in-depth medical and developmental history, including elements that were present throughout pregnancy and the postpartum period, will be taken into consideration.

Observation: The professionals will watch the youngster interact with others, as well as observe their behaviour and communication abilities.

Standardized Tests: There are a variety of standardized evaluations that can be utilized in order to determine the developmental stages and social communication abilities of the youngster.

Interviews with Parents: The information provided by parents and other carers is extremely significant. They are able to give valuable insight into the growth and behaviour of the child when they are at home.

Team Approach: The diagnosis of autism frequently requires the participation of a team approach, in which a group of specialists cooperate in order to produce an appropriate evaluation.

Finding Your Way Through the Emotional Landscape

The process of arriving at a diagnosis can be mentally and emotionally taxing on the individual's parents and carers. It's not uncommon to feel a range of emotions, ranging from worry and perplexity to relief and acceptance of the situation. It is essential to keep in mind that a diagnosis is not a label but rather a tool that can facilitate understanding and assistance for the individual receiving it.

In the chapters that are to follow, we will discuss how to manage the complexity of raising a child with autism, as well as how to access the resources and therapies that can help children with autism succeed. In addition to this, we will delve into the lives of autistic individuals and their families in order to shed light on the distinctive perspectives and qualities that autism contributes to our world.

However, for the time being, we should acknowledge that early warning signs are not dead ends but rather stepping stones on a path to self-discovery and development, and this applies to the child as well as the people who care about and are there for them.

Chapter 3: The autistic experience

In order to have a genuine acceptance of autism on our part, we need to make an effort to comprehend the realities that autistic people face on a daily basis. In this chapter, we take an in-depth look at the world of autism from the point of view of individuals who live within it. We get an understanding of the obstacles that autistic people face as well as the joys that they experience by examining the world through the eyes of autistic people and interacting with them.

Putting Oneself in Their Position and Observing the World from Their Perspective

People with autism perceive the world in a manner that is both fascinating and unique in comparison to the perspective held by neurologists. Oftentimes, sensory experiences, social relationships, and forms of communication will each take on their own distinctive dimensions.

Imagine living in a world where the fluttering of fluorescent lights is transformed into a mesmerizing dance, where the feel of fabrics against the skin is transformed into a sensory symphony, and where the minute changes in facial expressions communicate vast amounts of information. This is the world that a significant number of autistic people call home.

Sensory Sensitivities: Autism is characterized by a predisposition for sensory sensitivities. Some people find that the world is too much for them to handle since the sights, sounds, and textures are all heightened to an intensity that is unsettling. On the other hand, some people with autism actively seek out sensory stimulation, and these people discover that engaging in repetitive movements or being in places rich in sensory input brings them comfort and joy.

Difficulties with Communication: Autistic people often have a difficult time communicating, but they also have their own set of skills that set them apart from other people. Some people may have trouble communicating verbally, but they may excel in other forms of non-verbal communication, such as through the arts, music, or technology. It's possible that some people communicate with one another through non-verbal methods, such as sign language or enhanced communication equipment.

Understanding Meltdowns and Shutdowns
Meltdowns: Intense emotional outbursts can occur in autistic individuals when sensory inputs become overpowering, when confronted with intense emotions, or when the individual is forced to deal with a change in their routine. On the other hand, some people may enter a state of shutdown, during which they turn inward and retreat from the world as a method of self-regulation.

The Autistic Mind; A Novel Point of View: Thinking for autistic people can be exquisitely complex and laser-like in its attention to detail. A significant number of autistic people have an extraordinary capacity to identify patterns and particulars that are often overlooked by other people. This one-of-a-kind approach to thinking has resulted in important contributions being made to a variety of sectors, including mathematics, science, the arts, and technology.

Seeing Society Through the Eyes of an Autistic Person: One of the primary objectives of gaining

knowledge of what it is like to have autism is to become
aware of the ways in which society can become more
accepting and accommodating. We can cultivate
situations in which autistic people are able to flourish and
make full contributions if we recognize and value the
distinctive viewpoints and strengths autistic people
possess.

As we move on with our examination of autism in the
chapters to come, we will dig into many methods that can
be utilized to provide assistance and empowerment to
autistic individuals, as well as construct communities that
are inclusive and celebrate neurodiversity. We may
construct a path of empathy, acceptance, and appreciation
of the great range of human experiences if we put
ourselves in the position of people who have autism and
put ourselves in their shoes.

Chapter 4: The Autism Spectrum in Childhood

For all children, childhood is a time filled with wonder, growth, and discovery; autistic children are no exception to this rule. In this chapter, we delve into the distinctive experiences that autistic children have and investigate the various ways in which parents, carers, and educators can provide the support and understanding that is necessary for autistic children to flourish.

How to Foster a Child's Individuality: Caring for an Autistic Child

The experience of raising a child with autism may be equally gratifying and difficult. It is a journey full of moments of joy, discovery, and love; nevertheless, it may also include navigating uncertainty and seeking resources to support the particular needs of your kid.

Intervention and Therapies at an Early Age

Support for autistic children should begin as early as possible with intervention programs. The results of numerous studies have demonstrated that an accurate diagnosis and prompt intervention can have a substantial impact on the growth of a kid. It is common practice to assist autistic children in gaining important abilities in communication, social interaction, and daily functioning through the use of therapies such as Applied Behaviour Analysis (ABA), speech therapy, and occupational therapy.

However, intervention is only one part of the equation; as important is the development of a child's unique abilities and passions. Whether it's a preoccupation with a knack for art or a profound love of music, autistic children may have intense passions and abilities that may be appreciated and nurtured.

Creating a Community That Will Support One Another

Developing a support system is often necessary while caring for a child with autism. Developing relationships with other parents, support groups, and organizations that advocate for people with autism can give a plethora of information, resources, and emotional support. It is via these ties that parents are able to gain knowledge from the experiences of one another, discuss techniques, and celebrate the accomplishments of their children.

Education That Is Inclusive: In recent years, there has been an increasing emphasis on education that is inclusive, in which children with autism are educated along with their peers who are neurotypical. Inclusion not only benefits the autistic child by building social skills and offering role models, but it also benefits the classroom environment by promoting empathy, understanding, and diversity.

Celebrations and Struggles: Childhood is full of both, and children with autism are no different. Milestones mark the passage of time, and so do struggles. They may experience particular challenges in a variety of domains, including communication, social interactions, and sensitivity to sensory input. However, it is essential to keep in mind that these obstacles may be conquered with enough patience, comprehension, and the right kind of assistance.

It is also a time to celebrate the wins that have been achieved, regardless of how insignificant these achievements may appear to others. For a child with autism, seemingly insignificant milestones, such as uttering their first word, successfully interacting with a peer, or expressing themselves creatively, can mean the world.

In the following pages, we will examine the course that autism takes through adolescence and maturity, the role that carers play, and the significance of inclusive schooling. However, for the time being, let us not forget that childhood is a time of awe, development, and possibility for all children, including those on the autistic spectrum.

Chapter 5: Autism During the Teenage Years and into Adulthood

As autistic people go from childhood into adolescence and then adulthood, they confront a distinct set of difficulties and opportunities that are specific to their stage of life. In this chapter, we examine the ever-changing experiences of autistic teenagers and adults, including their educational and occupational routes, as well as their road towards independence and self-advocacy.

Challenges and Opportunities Associated with the Transition to Adolescence

For all people, adolescence is a time of significant change; however, for autistic adolescents, this stage of life can present a unique blend of opportunities for adventure, personal growth, and struggle. It is absolutely necessary to provide the required support and understanding to them as they navigate the challenging waters of puberty.

Education and Work Opportunities

When it comes to education, the transition from elementary school to middle school and high school can be especially difficult for many autistic adolescents. Alterations to daily routines, shifts in social expectations, and increased academic pressures could call for more support. It is critical to collaborate with teachers in order to develop individualized education programmes (IEPs) for students that take into account their specific challenges and opportunities.

Considerations concerning employment are frequently part of the process of making the shift from youth to adulthood. Adults with autism have a wide variety of skills and talents to offer the workforce, yet they may also experience challenges such as interview anxiety or sensitivity to sensory input. When it comes to assisting persons with autism in finding meaningful employment, programmes that provide vocational training, job coaching, and workplace modifications can be of tremendous assistance.

Self-Representation and Autonomous Living Skills

When autistic people reach adulthood, one of their most common goals is to live freely and be able to make their own decisions. It's possible that during the adventure, they'll pick up useful life skills like how to cook, manage money, and navigate around town. In addition, it is also important to cultivate self-advocacy abilities in individuals so that they may successfully communicate their requirements and preferences.

Relationships and social connections are something that needs to be navigated.

For autistic teens and adults, navigating social connections can remain a challenging endeavour throughout their lives. It's possible that they'll need more guidance and assistance while they work to build and sustain their connections, whether they're romantic, familial, or friendships. Nevertheless, many autistic people are able to have meaningful and satisfying relationships, and it is imperative that we acknowledge their achievements in this domain.

Advocacy and Participation in Community Activities

Many people who have autism reach maturity and, as a result, become ardent advocates for themselves and their community. They might become members of advocacy organizations, take part in self-advocacy groups, or get involved in activism in order to raise awareness of autism and encourage acceptance of those with the condition.

Honouring Accomplishments and Individual Differences

It is essential to recognize and honour the special accomplishments and qualities that autistic people possess throughout a person's childhood, youth, and maturity. Autistic adults make significant contributions to society in a variety of ways, whether it is through the pursuit of higher education, the achievement of professional success, or the improvement of their local community.

In the chapters to come, we will proceed with our investigation of various ways for empowerment, inclusive education, and the significance of recognizing the value of neurodiversity. We intend to cultivate a society that recognizes and honours the contributions made by all of its members, regardless of the neurodiversity of those members, as we travel through the varied experiences that autistic individuals have throughout the course of their lifetimes.

Chapter 6: The work of carers.

Carers are incredibly important in the lives of autistic individuals because they provide support, direction, and love throughout the autistic person's journey. In this chapter, we discuss the specific problems that carers experience, the significance of practising self-care, and the complexity of sibling relationships in families that include people who have autism.

A Voyage of Love and Support for Those in Need

Caring for a family member who has autism may be a journey that is both intensely rewarding and frequently taxing for the parents, siblings, and extended family members involved. Carers go through a journey of love, advocacy, and resiliency as they serve as nurturers, educators, and champions for their autistic family members.

Striking a Balance Between Caring for Oneself and Others

It is crucial to keep in mind that self-care is not a luxury but rather a need while taking on the position of a carer because it can be an all-encompassing responsibility. Self-compassion and taking the time to refuel are essential practices for carers, as is reaching out to family, friends, and community organizations for assistance. When those providing care put their own health and happiness first, they are in a better position to deliver the care and support that their loved ones require.

Relationships between Siblings and Their Dynamics
Many times, autistic individuals' siblings go through experiences that are one of a kind. They could have to deal with difficulties, such as adjusting to changes in the routines and dynamics of the family, or they might take on new responsibilities, such as being their autistic sibling's protectors and champions. On the other hand, these connections have the potential to be extremely significant and productive, promoting empathy, patience, and comprehension.

Help and Sources of Information for Carers
Carers are also in need of support. Families of autistic individuals have access to a wide variety of organizations and resources that are devoted to giving them assistance, information, and emotional support. Developing relationships with these organizations and other carers can

provide opportunities to gain insightful knowledge and a sense of belonging in a community.

Honouring the Struggles and Triumphs of Caregiving
The journey of a carer is one that is filled with both victories and difficulties. It is a credit to the love and dedication of carers that each milestone achieved, no matter how insignificant, is attained. It is crucial to celebrate these accomplishments, to honour the hard work and sacrifices that have been made, and to recognize that the role of the carer is essential in the growth and well-being of autistic individuals.

In the chapters that follow, we will proceed with our examination of several methods that can be utilized to provide autistic individuals with assistance and empowerment, to construct communities that are welcoming to all, and to celebrate neurodiversity. It is necessary to keep in mind that carers are not alone as we traverse the many facets of autism; together, we can make the world a more accepting and compassionate place for all people. As we continue on this road, it is important to remember that.

Chapter 7: Inclusive Education and Society

When it comes to the lives of autistic people, inclusive education is more than just a philosophy; it's a powerful force that can bring about positive change. In this chapter, we explore deeper into the necessity of inclusive education as well as the broader implications of an inclusive society that fosters acceptance and celebrates variety.

Developing Educational Spaces That Are Open to All Students

Every student, regardless of their skills or impairments, has the right to learn and grow in an atmosphere that is supportive and inclusive, and this is the foundation upon which inclusive education is based. This allows autistic kids to have access to a curriculum that caters to their specific requirements and areas of expertise, in addition to providing them with opportunities for social contact and learning from their peers.

Promoting Acceptance in Educational Institutions
Not only do inclusive schools make room for students on the autism spectrum, but they also encourage an environment that is accepting and respectful of others. Schools have the ability to foster an environment in which differences are embraced rather than stigmatized if they take steps to educate students' classmates about autism and encourage empathy.

Promoting an Inclusive Environment Outside of the Classroom
Inclusion is not limited to the confines of a school setting; rather, it permeates all aspects of a community. When it comes to the formation of an inclusive society, businesses, organizations, and communities all have a part to play. This entails offering autistic people chances for employment, making public areas and services accessible, and accommodating their needs in any way possible.

Combating Stigmas and Stereotypes
The stigmas and assumptions that have frequently surrounded autism are challenged by inclusive education as well as by an inclusive society on a broader scale. We may work towards dispelling myths and promoting a

more accurate and positive understanding of autism if we acknowledge and value the contributions of autistic individuals.

Advocacy and Policy Development

The cause of inclusive education and an inclusive society can move forward significantly due to the work of advocates. We have the ability to build a world in which everyone has the chance to live up to their full potential if we advocate for policies and practices that are inclusive on all levels, including the local, national, and international levels.

Honouring the Neurodiversity of People

The concept that neurological abnormalities, such as autism, are inherent variations of the human experience is at the heart of the celebration of neurodiversity that lies at the foundation of an inclusive society. Embracing neurodiversity is a step beyond merely tolerating people of different mental states; it is a step towards genuine acceptance and an appreciation of the complex tapestry that is the human mind.

In the chapters that follow, we will proceed with our examination of various ways to foster acceptance, develop communities that are welcoming to autistic people, and empower autistic individuals. As we continue on our path towards a more accepting society, one of our primary goals is to ensure that the tenets of inclusion and acceptance are not merely platitudes but rather the bedrock principles upon which our community will be built in the years to come.

Chapter 8: Embracing Autism: Stories of Hope and Inspiration

In every chapter of this book, we have discussed the many different aspects of autism, ranging from the first indications and symptoms to the process of diagnosis, as well as the works of carers and the significance of inclusive education. Now, we are going to turn our attention to stories, specifically those of hope, resiliency, and the unbreakable spirit of the human race. These are the experiences of autistic persons and their families who have tackled the obstacles of autism with courage and tenacity and who have inspired us to accept autism for everything it is.

A Collection of Personal Narratives from Autistic People

Those who have experienced the events being recounted often provide the most compelling narratives. In this part of the article, we hear from autistic people who talk about their lives, including the challenges they face and the successes they achieve. These first-person accounts offer a window into the multifaceted and dynamic world of autism. They debunk common misconceptions about autistic people and highlight the remarkable fortitude and resiliency that autistic people possess.

Advocates and Pioneers in Innovation
Individuals with autism and those who support them have made major contributions to our understanding of autism and to our attempts to create a world that is more welcoming to people with disabilities. We honour the activists who work persistently to increase awareness, promote acceptance, and support policy reforms that benefit the community of people with autism. We would also like to extend our gratitude to the pioneers whose distinctive points of view have been instrumental in advancing the fields of science, technology, and the arts.

Altering One's Perspectives
The accounts that are provided in this chapter serve as a timely reminder that having autism is not an impediment to leading a happy and meaningful life; rather, it is a component of the varied and colourful fabric that is human variation. Our goal is to foster a culture that is more welcoming and inclusive by encouraging empathy and challenging preconceived notions through the sharing of these personal tales.

As we move forward, may these tales serve as both a wellspring of motivation and an illustration of the untapped potential that is within each one of us. Autism is not an illness that has to be treated or a mystery that needs to be unravelled; rather, it is an essential component of the human experience that deserves to be comprehended, accepted, and celebrated.

In the chapters that are to come, we will look into several methods that can be utilized to provide autistic individuals with support and empowerment, to construct communities that are welcoming to all, and to promote neurodiversity. For the time being, however, let us take a moment to celebrate the uplifting and thought-provoking tales that serve to highlight the strength and beauty of the human spirit.

Chapter 9: Strategies for Empowerment

The empowerment of autistic people is not merely a destination; rather, it is a process that involves understanding, support, and celebration. In this chapter, we discuss a variety of approaches that can assist autistic individuals in thriving, constructing meaningful lives, and contributing their one-of-a-kind abilities to the wider world.

Improving One's Capacity for Effective Communication

The ability to communicate effectively is the cornerstone of empowerment. There is a high probability that many autistic people may experience difficulties with verbal communication; however, there are a great many alternative modes of communication that can be examined. Augmentative and alternative communication (AAC) devices, sign language, and visual assistance are some examples of these. The capacity of an individual to express themselves and form connections with others can be improved by adapting their modes of communication to meet their own requirements.

Environments That Are Pleasant to the Senses

It is vital to create environments that are hospitable to sensory input in order to reduce sensory overload and provide autistic individuals with a space that is more comfortable and welcoming for them. To accommodate a person's sensory sensitivities, this may require making adjustments to the lighting, sound levels, and other sensory stimuli. A well-planned layout has the potential to create a big impact in settings such as classrooms, workplaces, and public areas.

Developing essential life skills while fostering independency

Helping autistic people gain abilities that are useful in everyday life is another component of empowerment. Teaching skills necessary for daily living, such as cooking, cleaning, and budgeting, may fall under this category. These abilities not only encourage independent living but they also increase one's sense of pride and self-assurance.

Promoting the Use of Various Accommodations

Advocacy is a potent instrument that can be used to empower others. It is possible to have a significant impact by supporting people in their efforts to become their own advocates and assisting them in securing the required accommodations in their places of learning and employment. Individuals who are autistic should have equal access to opportunities and should not be held back by hurdles, and advocacy can help make that happen.

Fostering Acceptance and Inclusion as a Goal

The task of promoting inclusion and acceptance within communities and across society as a whole falls on all of us collectively. One way to make the world a more welcoming place for autistic people is to raise awareness of neurodiversity and acknowledge the one-of-a-kind contributions made by autistic people. It is possible to adopt measures in order to make sure that educational institutions, places of employment, and public areas are inclusive and accessible to everyone.

Approach That Is Centered on Strengths

A strategy that is centred on an individual's skills, interests, and talents takes into account those qualities and then builds upon them. We are better able to assist autistic people in reaching their full potential if we concentrate on what they are capable of doing rather than dwelling on the constraints they face.

Availability of Different Support Services

The availability of support services is absolutely necessary for empowerment. These services could include counselling, training for a specific job, or help with mental health issues. It is critical for the success of autistic individuals to ensure that these services are not only offered but also easily accessible.

These tactics for empowerment can serve as a road map for individuals, families, educators, and society as we continue our journey through the varied experiences of autism. We can make the world a more welcoming and enabling place for everyone if we put these methods into action and embrace the concepts of understanding, acceptance, and celebration of neurodiversity.

Chapter 10: Looking Ahead: Towards a Future That Is More Inclusive

Exploration, comprehension, and joy have characterized our trip along the spectrum of autism that we have been experiencing. In this final chapter, we turn our focus to the future, a future that holds the promise of a society that is more tolerant and inclusive of autistic people and all members of the neurodiversity community as a whole.

Combating Stigmas and Stereotypes

We need to face and challenge the stigmas and preconceptions that have been surrounding autism for a much longer period of time in order to create a future that is more inclusive. This includes developing a more sympathetic and informed public dialogue regarding autism, as well as spreading correct information and debunking myths about the condition.

Advocacy and Policy Development

Change is driven in large part by advocacy efforts. We may contribute to the development of a more just and fair future for people with autism if we advocate for policies that encourage inclusion, access to services, and accommodations. In the context of these efforts, collaboration with legislative bodies, educational institutions, and other influential members of the community may play a role in ensuring that the rights and requirements of autistic individuals are prioritized and recognized.

Honouring the Neurodiversity of People

The notion of neurodiversity is one that is fundamental to an inclusive vision of the future. We recognize that neurological variances, such as autism, are natural variations of the human experience. This is what we mean when we say that we are celebrating neurodiversity. This viewpoint inspires us to recognize and appreciate the distinct advantages and points of view that people with neurodiversity contribute to our communities and to society as a whole, and it encourages us to do so.

Education and an Awareness Effort

The most important forces driving change are education and awareness. It is possible for us to cultivate environments that promote the full involvement and contribution of autistic individuals if we work to increase understanding and acceptance of autism in educational institutions, businesses, and public spaces.

Self-Recovery as a Means of Personal Empowerment

Self-advocacy is the first step towards achieving empowerment. It is crucial for autistic people to be encouraged to find their voices, communicate their needs, and advocate for themselves. Doing so will help them achieve autonomy and success. Individuals who are equipped with the skills necessary for self-advocacy are better able to navigate a world that does not always comprehend or accommodate their particular requirements.

Community and a Sense of Belonging

Creating communities that are welcoming to people of all backgrounds takes continual work. It entails the creation of environments and support networks in which people with autism can interact with one another, socialize, and feel as though they belong somewhere. Diversity contributes to the wealth and vitality of the communities that recognize its value and accept it.

The Beauty that Comes from Diversity
Let us never lose sight of the wonderful things that diversity has to offer as we work towards a future that is more welcoming to all. Our world is made better, our perspectives are pushed further, and new ideas are spawned because of the diversity that exists among us. Let us, as we move forward, incorporate the knowledge and experiences that we have gained from this trip into our day-to-day lives, our neighbourhoods, and our society as a whole.

We can make the world a more accepting and compassionate place by embracing autism and celebrating the full spectrum of human neurodiversity. This will allow us to build a future in which every person, regardless of their neurodiversity, is appreciated, supported, and given the opportunity to fulfil their full potential.

As we come to the end of our trip, may we be able to take with us the spirit of understanding, acceptance, and celebration of neurodiversity. In doing so, we may ensure that the promise of a future that is more welcoming for everyone becomes a reality.

Conclusion

Our voyage through the spectrum of autism has been one filled with discovery, compassion, and enlightenment at every turn. We have navigated the many landscapes of autism, guided by a commitment to understanding, acceptance, and celebration of neurodiversity. From the early indicators and diagnosis to the stories of hope and inspiration, we have covered a wide range of topics related to autism.

As we have found out, autism is not a problem that can be solved, nor is it a condition that can be improved. It is a one-of-a-kind manifestation of the human experience, a distinct variation in the harmonious interplay of minds that makes our world more interesting. We have embraced autism across these pages for all that it is, which is to say that it is a complicated, lively, and delightfully diverse tapestry.

We have discussed the importance of carers, the trials and tribulations faced by autistic people throughout childhood, adolescence, and adulthood, as well as the benefits that can be gained through attending inclusive schools and living in communities. We have discussed the significance of advocacy, the advantages of self-advocacy, and the prospects for a future that is more welcoming to all people.

As part of our effort to normalize autistic people and their experiences, we have fought against negative stereotypes, acknowledged the many positive attributes that autistic people possess, and lobbied for policies that give priority to the rights and requirements of autistic people. As a result of our research, we know that it is possible to cultivate understanding, acceptance, and empathy in order to fashion conditions in which autistic people can flourish, contribute, and discover their own voices.

As we come to the end of this voyage, let us remember to take the knowledge and experiences we've gathered with us. Let us not forget that autism is not a restriction but rather a unique viewpoint, offering new ways of thinking, seeing, and being in the world. Let us also not forget that autism is not a limitation but rather a distinct perspective. Let's keep fighting against stereotypes, fighting for inclusiveness, and celebrating neurodiversity.

In the end, our objective is not simply to accept people with autism; rather, we want to accept the astonishing diversity of human minds. We want to do this because we recognize that every person, regardless of the neurodiversity they exhibit, has an important part to play in the magnificent fabric of mankind.

It is my hope that, as we move forward, we will be able to bring the spirit of neurodiversity awareness, acceptance, and celebration into our day-to-day lives, our communities, and our society. May we work together to create a world in which each and every person, irrespective of where they lie on the spectrum, is appreciated, supported, and given the opportunity to shine brilliantly.

The journey towards autism acceptance is an ongoing one, but it is a trip that is worth pursuing because it is a journey of love, acceptance, and a brighter, more inclusive future for everyone.